WRITING LINKS

WRITING LINKS

GRAMMAR IN STUDIES OF SOCIETY AND THE ENVIRONMENT

Love, Christine
Writing links: grammar in studies of society and the environment

ISBN 1 875622 35 7

I. English Language – Composition and exercises.
2. English Language – Study and teaching.
3. English language – Grammar – Study and teaching
I. Rushton, Kathleen, 1950- . II. Title.

428.2

First published April 2000

Laura Street Newtown NSW 2042 Australia
Book design by Stephen Goddard Design
Edited by Rosamund Else-Mitchell
Typeset in Times by Oracle Desktop Design
Printed by Star Printery
21 Coulson Street, Erskineville, NSW.

TABLE OF CONTENTS

ACKNOWLEDGEMENTS

We would like to thank Helen Empacher and Stephen Seiver and their families for the generosity and kindness they have shown in sharing their personal stories with us. It is a privilege to share the story of an indigenous person because it is truly part of the story of our country.

Current indigenous protocols required that the involvement of the indigenous community is encouraged in any discussion about Aboriginal culture in an educational context. The stories told here are related with the permission of the individuals involved but in any other case we would have contacted our local branch of the Aboriginal Educational Consultative Group (AECG) to seek advice.

Thank you also to all the work by members of the PETA Publications Committee in providing feedback and assisting with the redrafting process. Thank you also to Stephen Goddard for the delightful design and to the children whose artwork is included on the cover.

We would also like to acknowledge:

4M Lutheran Primary School, Wagga Wagga, NSW for reproduction of their class collage 'Celebrating older people in the community'.

Taylor Fuda, 7 years old of Holy Trinity Lutheran School, Mildura for reproduction of his painting 'Our River'.

NRMA for permission to reproduce extracts from the Clean Air 2000 Kit.

The Global Education Resource produced by AUSAID, UNICEF, World Vision and the NSW Department of School Education.

INTRODUCTION

The need to address literacy in all curriculum areas is apparent, and if we are to help students meet the rapidly increasing demands made on them in modern educational contexts we need to be able to focus on the language demands related to every area of learning. The development of writing through the identification of the structure of texts, and the deconstruction, modelling and joint construction of texts-types is now an accepted pedagogical practice and is becoming more widespread. However, students need to recognise and be able to transfer their knowledge of the basic structures and staging of text-types from curriculum area to curriculum area. Whether students are native speakers, or learning English as a second language, making explicit certain aspects of effective writing can only be an advantage in developing both reading and writing.

SPOKEN AND WRITTEN LANGUAGE

By choosing to foreground language in all areas of learning a teacher can show which language choices are appropriate for a range of text-types with a variety of purposes and audiences. Students' knowledge of the staging and sequencing of text-types according to their societal purpose also helps them as *readers* to anticipate the content of a particular text and access the information more readily within it (Derewianka 1990; Unsworth 1993). The complexity of techniques of cohesion, the use of more formal registers and of technical vocabulary are some of the problems students experience when writing non-fiction texts (Wray & Lewis 1997).

Students who are less successful in generating their own texts often tend to reproduce spoken language in their writing. Even if they have some understandings about the staging and structure of the genre in which they are writing, they tend to rely heavily on the spoken mode which may not be appropriate for the text's purpose and audience. In some genres it is easier for students to make the transition from the spoken to the written mode, as in a procedure, for example, where the spoken and written genres are more aligned. However, when producing other genres or text-types, particularly non-fiction text-types, it seems to be much harder and students often incongruently use the spoken mode or "written down talk". Students can be assisted in developing the types of generalisations about writing structures and text expectations that go beyond the genre or the individual piece of writing which they are constructing. This learning can be facilitated if students are taught to ask what appropriate language choices suit the purpose, subject matter and audience of both spoken and written texts.

In his discussion of the differences between spoken and written language, Halliday (1985: 81) says that written language presents events as *products*, but spoken language represents them as *processes*. This is a central difference between written and spoken language modes. Most teachers will have noted that students are more easily able to retell events in a recount than they are to use the techniques of nominalisation or the passive voice which are often used in scientific or bureaucratic writing. For example, we are more likely to say "The ship dumped oil in the sea " than we are "An oil spill polluted the sea".

However, students can rely on their oral language as a resource for planning and writing if teachers then make explicit the language structures, stages and features of texts and support students in constructing these texts. Thus speaking and listening activities can complement writing and reading tasks to assist students to build their knowledge and understanding.

As teachers we all recognise those students who have a "natural" ability with language but it is no coincidence that the ethnic and socioeconomic groups who have the "most natural ability" are often the ones whose spoken discourse is more like written discourse. Of course, almost no-one, "talks" like a book but some people are able to switch from everyday conversation to the kind of talk which sounds more like writing; the formal talk of the lecture, the sermon, the specific instruction. This ability to switch is really the ability to choose language that best serves to communicate to a specific audience the purpose which the speaker or writer has chosen. The language choices a student makes when creating texts are always a reflection of prior learning and a wider range, or more appropriate choices can be taught and learned.

In practice this means that teachers need to teach English or literacy skills in all Learning Areas to support students to make appropriate language choices when writing and talking about the subject matter or field. "It is now well-known that each subject has its own way of using language to develop knowledge and understandings relevant to that area. The language of science, for example, is quite different from the language of history. The language used in English literary texts is quite different from that of mathematics texts. Students need to be able to read and write texts which become increasingly technical and subject-specific as they move through the school system from primary to high school." (Derewianka 1998: 5).

Each chapter of *Writing Links* takes as its English focus one aspect of language or a grammatical feature that was determined by the demands of the tasks, generally writing or speaking tasks, in the studies of Society and Environment activities. In this way students can be explicitly alerted to the language choices available in this context, and use suitable genres and vocabulary for the purpose and audience of the task. To assist students as they practise using language we have provided a range of lists, handouts, scaffolds and activity sheets. These can be made into wall charts, used for joint constructions, modelling texts or handed out to students directly.

TERMINOLOGY AND METALANGUAGE

To help students develop the understandings which will support appropriate use of the resources of language in different Learning Areas, we must be able to help them develop ways of talking about language itself, ie a *metalanguage*. In an educational context any English syllabus employs terminology which can be used to help students *learn about* language. Many of us have not formally learnt any terminology for talking about language and there is a great deal of confusion about terms like 'functional grammar', 'traditional grammar', 'prescriptive grammar'.

The most simple explanation is to consider all terminology as referring to one of two perspectives on language – *function* or *class*. *Function* refers to how the language is working in context, what it is being used to do, and *class* is just that, the naming of a word or group of words by type. The following example is simple and easy to remember, whatever terminology is being used.

	I	*love*	*you*
Function	participant	mental process	participant
Class	pronoun	verb	pronoun

These two ways of looking at language are not mutually exclusive but rather, they are complementary as one categorises (*class*) and the other describes (*function*).

In some syllabus documents terms such as 'sensing verbs' or 'feeling verbs' are used to indicate both class and function. However in most reference books on language, verbs are only considered in terms of class eg *auxiliary*, *main* or *modal* and the forms they take in different tenses. Only a functional approach is concerned with the patterns of language in texts and how language functions to construct meaning. Therefore, a functional approach may employ all the terms which define *class*, but will also use terminology which refers to what meaning is produced in what context, the *function*. For example, a book such as *A Grammar Companion for Primary Teachers* by Beverly Derewianka focusing on a functional approach refers to *auxiliary, main* and *modal* verbs and also uses terminology to show how verbal groups function in texts eg *material, mental, verbal* and *relational processes*. *A Grammar Companion, Exploring How Texts Work* also by Derewianka and John Collerson's *Grammar in Teaching*, all published by PETA will provide valuable further support for many of these activities.

WRITING LINKS

This book is an endeavour to develop units of work in the primary school with a focus on both English and Studies of Society and Environment. The definitions used for these Learning Areas have been taken from *English: A curriculum profile for Australian schools* and *Studies of Society and Environment: A curriculum profile for Australian schools* both produced by the Australian Education Council as a joint project between all the States and Territories and the Commonwealth. While the content of the subject area English causes little confusion, the other Learning Area in question is variously referred to as Human Society and its Environment, Social Studies and Studies of Society and the Environment, but inevitably it includes studies which traditionally have been known as history and geography. In most cases the latter now includes environmental studies. The subject area now reflects the history of the Australian nation which includes the history of its indigenous peoples and the diverse, multicultural nature of Australian society today. In using the name Studies of Society and the Environment, and alluding to the national document we are sure that these units will resonate with all primary teachers in Australia.

Studies of Society and Environment has a content focus which includes culture and its diversity in the Australian context. As language both *defines* culture, and, is at the same time a continually changing *product* of culture, there is an obvious connection between the development of reflective thinking about language use and its relationship to the communities reflected in the classroom or wider society. The ability to think reflectively about language and to make informed choices about its use will support students in their understandings about the content of both English and Studies of Society and Environment which requires the student to describe, report, explain, analyse, persuade, discuss and evaluate aspects of culture. The text-types prominent in this Learning Area are powerful genres in our society and as Martin and Rothery argue (1980, 1981, 1986), they offer students access to the 'language of power' and thus access to becoming active, functioning members of society.

In *Writing Links*, we have included or referred to resources that are accessible to almost all Australian teachers, and where possible we have used resources that have been provided free to schools such as complimentary kits, videos and materials. Further suggestions appear in the Resources section at the end of each chapter. This book can be used flexibly, even if specific resources cannot be found. As English and Studies of Society and Environment are two separate fields (or subjects), each chapter has an overview of the skills and understandings covered in the unit, as well as a topics matrix which shows the content and skills focus for each topic. The two topics in each unit can stand alone as they have their own references, Handouts and Activity Sheets. Of course, any activity which requires reading, writing, talking or listening obviously requires English skills, however, the explicit focus for each unit is on a grammatical feature which can be contextualised, explained, scaffolded, modelled and practised for the purpose of the speaking and writing tasks in each teaching and learning sequence.

CHAPTER 1
AUSTRALIAN PEOPLE AND PLACES

RATIONALE

This unit has as its focus the study of people and places recognises that Australia's international image is based on these elements. Study of people provides an opportunity for students to learn from human interactions and achievements. Students learn to value the achievements of individuals in the contexts of the ethnic and cultural groups of which they are members. Students understand the contribution these individuals and groups have made to Australia's cultural and economic development. Study of places assists students in learning about natural and built environments and how they should be managed to ensure sustainability. Students also examine places in which they or others live, and why certain places have special significance for particular cultural and ethnic groups in Australia.

Students explore ways of talking and writing about Australia's history and geography and how to express the significance certain people and places have for Australians today. **Students jointly and independently construct a factual recount** of a significant Australian's life recognising and discussing the purpose of and audience for such a text. They **select information from a variety of sources to develop a fluent and informative summary** of the events and achievements in the life of a significant Australian. They are supported to **find ways of expressing a point of view** about Australia's built and natural environment and **to listen to and evaluate the opinions expressed by their peers**.

OVERVIEW OF SKILLS AND UNDERSTANDINGS

Studies of Society and Environment

- Identify significant Australian achievements
- Identify significant places
- Gather information about different viewpoints
- Describe and sequence events

English

- Participate in / listen to a discussion
- Participate in / evaluate a debate
- Develop noun groups in a description of a person, place or thing
- Plan writing, conference and redraft
- Write a factual recount
- Make notes for a discussion

TOPICS

Content	Sample Teaching and Learning Activities	Skills – Studies of Society and Environment	Skills – English
Topic 1 Australia's people and their achievements			
Study of prominent people in the arts, sport, science, history and politics.	Choose an Australian to study.	Selecting information.	Participating in a discussion – asking questions, offering information and cooperating with a group. Planning writing. Conferencing with a peer before redrafting.
Topic 2 Australia's significant places			
Study of significant places.	Compare significant Australian places and their importance for different groups.	Identifying significant places. Locating places and identifying their features.	Listening to / participating in a class debate. Evaluating / developing a point of view supported by reasons.

Topic 1 Australia's people and their achievements

Teaching and learning activities

1 In small groups choose one field of endeavour from the list below:

- the arts
- history
- sport
- politics
- science
- entertainment

2 Have each group use a selection of library resources to generate a list of Australians who have made significant achievements in each field. Keep the lists for further activities.

3 Students select an Australian from the lists made in Activity 1 and use library resources or the Internet to find out more about them. Explain to them that the research focus is to find information about who the person was, when and where they lived, what things they did that were significant and in what sequence. Students use **Activity Sheet 1.1** to record the information

4 Prepare for a class discussion in small mixed ability groups. Assign the roles of reporter and scribe to two students who will need the most support with this activity. Other students can be assigned the roles of encourager, organiser, summariser, clarifier or any role you think appropriate. Give each group one of the focus questions to discuss and encourage them to record their ideas. The group reporters can then begin the discussion by reporting back to the class.

Focus Questions

What features are common to most or all of the people you have researched? What features are the rarest? Are there more women than men? Is there any field with more women than others? Are there many Australians of Asian or Aboriginal descent? Are there any very young people? Why?

---

5 Choose THREE of the people selected by the students and provide three different source texts which convey information about them, eg

- a website page
- a taped interview
- an encyclopedia entry

6 **Activity Sheet 1.1** can be used by students to record the information in the three source materials. These texts can also be used to introduce and highlight *nouns* and *noun groups* (**Handout 1.3**) which they will be using in their factual recount.

7 Choose one of the Australians from the class list and have the whole class brainstorm information about their life (you will have to have facts such as dates etc to hand). Alternatively, have students find out one important piece of information about the person, and record where they found it, to ensure the factual input and substance of this activity.

8 As a whole class, jointly construct a factual recount of the significant events in that person's life. Model the structure of a factual recount text using **Handout 1.2** explaining grammatical features such as *noun groups* (See **Handout 1.3**) and *time connectives*.

9 Give out **Activity Sheet 1.4** which will provide a structure for planning and writing the factual recount.

10 In pairs or independently, students choose the Australian they have researched or another from the initial list. They will need to return to researching if they are studying someone different.

11 Once they have their factual content, students need to develop a range of *noun groups* to describe the person and to write a factual recount. **Handout 1.3** provides some suggestions for *noun groups* and can be also be used as a wall chart. You may want students to brainstorm additional words. They could begin with people well-known to them either locally or through television.

12 Students conference with a peer before redrafting their final copy, using the structure of the factual recount as their guideline. Peer editing can also include highlighting or underlining a language feature (eg all the *time connectives*). This way redrafting can be part of a particular learning focus for the lesson; less able students can be supported in improving their own and others texts.

13 If students each research a different Australian, they could work towards compiling all the factual recounts into an illustrated class book of Great Australians which could be used for related topics or historical studies.

Activity Sheet 1.1

Research for a Factual Recount

Name:

Date of birth:

Cultural or ethnic background:

Education:

Field:

Write some noun groups which give information about

The person:

Their ideas/achievements:

Describe their achievements:

Model of a Factual Recount

Robert Gordon Menzies

Sir Robert Gordon Menzies is Australia's longest serving Prime Minister. He was Prime Minister twice from 1939-1941 and then from 1949-1966. He was born in Victoria in 1894. By 1918 he was a barrister who wanted to enter politics. First he won a seat in the Victorian Parliament and then he became a member of the House of Representatives in Federal Parliament. He was Attorney-General before he became Prime Minister. He was Prime Minister when Australia entered World War II. He began the political party we now know as the Liberal Party of Australia. As its leader, Sir Robert Menzies is remembered as the one of Australia's most influential leaders and our longest serving Prime Minister.

Handout 1.3

Noun Groups

Noun Groups give information about people, places and things. They can be large or small but they must have at least a **noun**, a person, place or thing (eg Don Burke, the garden, a plant) or a **pronoun**, one of the words which stands in for a noun like it, I, you, he, she, we, they. In a factual recount your nouns will include the person you are writing about (eg *John Macarthur*) and some of the things they achieved (introduced Marino *sheep* into Australia).

Large noun groups usually include **adjectives**. Here are some adjectives which might help you describe the qualities of your chosen Australian and extend the noun groups in your factual recount.

Example

Caroline Chisholm was *compassionate*, *courageous* and *organised*.

Justice Lionel Murphy's changes to the legal system were *enlightened* and *fair*.

ardent
acute
adventurous
amusing
artistic
benevolent
bold
brave
capable
cheerful
clever
confident
considerate
courageous
creative
cultured
dedicated
defiant
demanding

determined
devoted
discriminating
distinguished
earnest
efficient
energetic
enlightened
enterprising
enthusiastic
equitable
even-handed
extravagant
fair
flexible
forthright
forward-thinking
friendly

generous
genial
gentle
good-humoured
hard-working
helpful
honest
idealistic
imaginative
impartial
important
influential
ingenious
inspirational
intellectual
intelligent
interesting
inventive

jovial
just
kind
lively
loyal
neighbourly
obliging
objective
open-minded
organised
original
outspoken
passionate
patient
poetic
polite
practical
progressive

realistic
reliable
resolute
resourceful
romantic
sensible
sincere
spirited
strategic
supportive
sympathetic
talented
thoughtful
trustworthy
unselfish
versatile
visionary
wise
zealous.

Activity Sheet 1.4

Factual Recount

Title:

Orientation

Who?

When?

Where?

Why?

Events (in time order – use conjunctions and time connectives to sequence events – first, then, next, after, as a result, during, since, meanwhile, until, as soon as)

-
-
-
-
-

Summary statement

Topic 2 Australia's significant places

Teaching and learning activities

1. As a class brainstorm the reasons why a place might be significant or special.

2. Using some of the ideas from the brainstorm, have students collect pictures of significant Australian places to make a classroom display. A range of magazines, newspapers and travel brochures will be useful resources. There should be a combination of built and natural places: cities, towns, the bush, farms, mines, the desert, rainforests, reefs etc.

3. Have students locate places shown in the display on a map of Australia (and/or your local area). Point out to students the symbols used on maps and what they represent (eg scale, size of lettering, lines and markers to represent capital cities, towns, roads, rail links, colours to represent landforms and water). Using information from the map (of the country or the local area) and appropriate symbols, students can draw their own maps adding other members of the class' significant places.

4. In pairs or small groups students discuss the significance of some of the following, or other significant local places, for indigenous and non-indigenous Australians, eg Uluru, Sydney Opera House, Kakadu National Park, student's place of birth/ their parents' place of birth, sacred site, church, mosque, synagogue, temple. Make sure these are also marked on the class map.

5. Write ideas from the class discussion under the heading "Significance for Indigenous and Non-Indigenous Australians". Use two columns and have each group write up and share their findings about each place.

6. In groups prepare for a debate about protecting Australia's heritage. Each group should think of reasons either 'for' or 'against' the topic "That places are important to people" to develop arguments about protecting our heritage, both built and natural.

7. Split the class in half to argue 'for' or 'against' the topic. In small groups each side should use **Activity Sheet 1.5** to assemble the reasons they have developed into a main argument, supporting arguments and examples.

8. Hold a class debate on "That places are important to people". This could involve the whole class speaking one after the other. Alternatively, three of four members of the class can be on one team and three or four on another. These groups will need some more preparation time to agree on their main argument, organise their supporting arguments and decide in which order they will speak.

9. The remainder of the class will share the adjudicator's job. Students can be organised into groups to encourage and evaluate those who are taking part in the debate (Pogulis 1998) and evaluate the speakers by recording comments next to these three headings:

Matter is concerned with the definition of the subject, facts and content used and how consistently either side of the debate can convince the audience of their viewpoint.

Manner refers to the body language, volume, intonation, gesture, eye contact, credibility and every aspect of the delivery of the speech.

Method is how the individual speaker, and the team organise and support their arguments, whether they use examples and how well the examples provide evidence for the arguments.

The debate might conclude with a vote to decide a winner based on the comments recorded by the class and/or a show of hands.

Activity Sheet 1.5

Planning a Debate

Topic:

Main Argument

Supporting argument

Examples

Supporting argument

Examples

Supporting argument

Examples

RESOURCES

(1998) *Discovering Democracy: Upper Primary Units*. Carlton, Vic: Curriculum Corporation.

(1998) *Discovering Democracy: Middle Primary Units*. Carlton, Vic: Curriculum Corporation.

(1998) *Discovering Democracy: Stories of Democracy*. (CD-ROM). Carlton, Vic: Curriculum Corporation.

(1998) *Discovering Democracy: Parliament at Work*. (CD-ROM). Carlton, Vic: Curriculum Corporation.

(1999) *Taking the initiative*. Department of Education and Training, Sydney: Arts Education Centre.

Carter, J (1981) *Nothing to Spare: Recollections of Australian Pioneer Women*. Ringwood, Vic: Penguin Books.

Children of the Murray-Darling Basin (1999) *Where We Live: Writing and Artwork*. Sydney: PETA in partnership with the Murray-Darling Basin Commission.

Coghill, L et al (1997) *Footprints: to country, kin and cultures.* Melbourne: Curriculum Corporation.

Crew, G & Tan S (1999) *Memorial*. Port Melbourne: Lothain.

Crew, G & Tan, S (1999) *Memorial.Victoria*: Lothain Books.

Curie, W & Adamson M (1997) *Women of Australia: Shaping our history*. South Melbourne: Macmillan.

Facey, B (1985) *A fortunate life*. Ringwood, Vic : Penguin Books.

Fox, M (1992) *Memories: An Autobiography*. Flinders Park, SA: Era Publications.

Gurry, Tim et al (1992) *The defence of Australia: An investigative resource kit. Rybuck Media and History* Teachers' Association of Victoria & Australian War Memorial.

Hardie, N, Rutherford, M & walsh, J (1993) *Investigating Our Society*. 2nd edition. Melbourne: Longman Cheshire.

Hill S & Hill T (1990) *The collaborative classroom.* Armadale Victoria: Eleanor Curtain Publishing.

Janeen, B (1994) *Amazing Landforms*. Flinders Park, SA: Era Publications.

McCowan J & Bell G (1992) *PEN 90 Learning difficulties and classroom support.* Sydney: PETA.

Nicholson J (1998) *Who's Running this Country?* Sydney: Allen & Unwin.

Pogulis V (1996) 'Talking to persuade: debating in the classroom' in Jones P (ed) *Talking to learn.* Sydney: PETA.

Robinson, P (1999) *This fantastic century Worksheets*. Queensland: Queensland Newspapers Pty Ltd.

www.hht.nsw.gov.au	Trust Houses
www.lgsa.org.au/edukit/home.htm	Local Government Education Kit
www.austrade.gov.au	Austrade
www.fed.gov.au/	Federal Governement Entry Point
www.nsw.gov.au/	NSW Governement
www.gov.info.au/	Australian Govenmenet Home Page
www.statistics.gov.au	Australian Bureau of Statistics

CHAPTER 2
AUSTRALIA'S MULTICULTURAL HERITAGE

RATIONALE

The study of Australia's diverse society has as its focus ways to develop understanding of the impact of cultural diversity within Australia. Studying the concept of multiculturalism extends beyond the celebration of differences in traditional cultural customs, to an understanding of the beliefs and lifestyles of the people of Australia. Through the study of multiculturalism as a perspective embedded in Studies of Society and Environment students will develop an understanding of Australia's cultural and linguistic diversity, both past and present.

Students will **elicit, or locate and select information from a variety of sources** using interviews and a range of information skills to build their knowledge and understanding of Australia's multicultural heritage. Students will **research and describe a custom or practice** of one cultural group in Australia and interview a member of that group. During this process students will consider the role of the interviewer and **how questions can best be formed to elicit the information desired**. They will also **write a biographical recount** of the interviewee's life and select important events to sequence logically. Students will **practise editing skills** with a focus on the use of a range of verbs. This will assist students to **write a biography** which reflects on the motivations and feelings of its subject as well as a sequence of events and actions.

OVERVIEW OF SKILLS AND UNDERSTANDINGS

Studies of Society and Environment

- Investigate identity and culture
- Examine the lives and cultural practices of a particular cultural group
- Discuss diverse viewpoints in our community
- Research using a variety of sources

English

- Define a research topic
- Examine the role of the interviewer and develop questions
- Make generalisations and predictions
- Identify different types of verbs
- Develop editing skills
- Write a factual description
- Write a biographical recount

TOPICS

Content	Sample Teaching and Learning Activities	Skills – Studies of Society and Environment	Skills – English
Topic 1 Indigenous Australians			
A study of two indigenous Australian families.	Investigate the role of language in defining identity. Examine the lives and viewpoints of some indigenous Australians. Develop an understanding of the contribution of indigenous Australians to Australian culture.	Investigating identity and culture. Examining the lives of particular groups of Australians. Investigating various aspects of culture. Discussing points of view about issues which shape Australian culture.	Examining the role of the interviewer. Eliciting information and developing precise questions. Using information to make generalisations and predictions. Identifying different types of verbs. Developing editing skills. Writing a biographical recount.
Topic 2 Multicultural Australia today			
A study of multicultural Australia today.	Examine news media articles which reflect the multicultural nature of Australia today. Explore images of what it is to be Australian.	Researching using news media articles and web sites. Developing images which reflect knowledge and understandings gained from research.	Defining a research topic and locating and selecting relevant information. Writing a factual description of a custom or celebration.

Topic 1 Indigenous Australians

Teaching and learning activities

1. Students survey classmates, teachers, and family about an important aspect of identity, culture and language. Their task is to find out a) what language(s) is/are spoken, b) what countries these languages are spoken in, and c) the importance of speaking a/the language from the home country and any reasons for the answer. Students could use the **Activity Sheet 2.1** for the survey.

2. Have students read the information in **Handout 2.3** to prepare for a class discussion about the Empacher family. The following questions can be used to explore ideas about the relationship between language and culture

---

?

Why does Helen say that Tazmann might only be able to learn about his culture from books? What do you think happened to the Yuin language? Is there more than one Aboriginal language? Why does Helen say "Education is the power for the future?"

---

3. Imagine that Tazmann is talking to his parents about his university studies. What choices has he made so far? Which country is he living in? What is he studying? Is he learning another language? What do both his parents feel about his choices? In small groups, students role play a discussion that the Empacher family might have in twenty years time. The groups can prepare for the role play by re-reading the interview with Helen and Jurgen. These words may help students make notes individually about the family's life to date and what might happen:

• identity	• culture	• past
• future	• Aboriginal	• Koori
• experience	• influence	

4. Distribute **Handout 2.4** on *verb types*. Explain to students that different types of verbs express different aspects of our experiences (eg doing, thinking, saying, relating). Using **Activity Sheet 2.5**, have students list all the different types of verbs in the text in **Handout 2.2**. The verbs are all in **bold print**.

5. Divide the class into TWO groups, then into an even number of pairs. Groups should read either the interview with Helen or the interview with Jurgen. Using Helen and Jurgen's answers as the starting point, each group should try to predict some of the questions that Helen and Jurgen were asked in the interview.

6. Organise the pairs predicting Helen's questions to join together and the pairs predicting Jurgen's to join together to put together two group lists of FIVE questions each. Encourage students to put the questions in the order they might have been asked and to ensure that each question has not been asked previously.

7. The larger groups should appoint two spokespeople each to report back to the whole class. One will read the questions and the other can read out the sentence(s) which answer the question. Combine all the questions on the board and write them up in one list of interview questions.

8. In small groups or individually have students use the final class list of questions to interview a friend or local resident who is a member of an indigenous or other cultural group in the local community. Use **Handout 2.6** to help students prepare for the interview and organise it appropriately.

9. Students can prepare a one minute oral presentation for the whole class based on the interview. Students can illustrate significant events in the person's life using a storyboard (see **Activity Sheet 2.7**) based on the interview, to provide a structure for the oral presentation. If their subjects are in agreement and can provide photos, these could be used instead of illustrations. A caption should be written under each picture which describes the significant event shown (eg Ty Qaio was married on 30 May 1985; Jennifer Biddle became a Senior Lecturer in Health Sciences at the University of Melbourne in 1998).

10. Distribute **Activity Sheet 2.9** which is a scaffold for a biographical recount. Students will write about the person they interviewed.

11. Cut up some copies of the biographical recount of Stephen Raymond Seiver (**Handout 2.8**) into sections. Explain to students the structural (eg orientation and concluding statements) and grammatical features (eg *time connectives*) as highlighted on the Handout. Have them reassemble the information in the correct sequence.

12. As a whole class jointly reconstruct the biographical recount of Stephen Raymond Seiver.

13. Individually and using the model as a guide, students write a recount of the life of their interviewee using information previously gathered and recorded in notes and on the storyboard.

14. In pairs students edit each other's first drafts by choosing a focus for editing and tracing this feature in the text, (eg the grammatical features such as a range of *verb types*, or *time connectives* used, or sequencing in the text).

Activity Sheet 2.1

Survey classmates, teachers, and family to see what languages they can speak. How many languages are spoken, and what countries do these languages come from? Is speaking the language from their home country important? Why or why not?

Name

Language(s) Spoken

Country of origin

Is it important to you to speak your own language? Why or why not?

Name

Language(s) Spoken

Country of origin

Is it important to you to speak your own language? Why or why not?

Handout 2.2

The Empacher family

The Empacher family live in Sydney where Tazmann Stevin Empacher was born in 1999. His mother Helen, who was also born in Sydney, is Aboriginal. His father Jurgen is of Austrian descent and grew up in Zimbabwe.

Jurgen: **I speak** English, it's my first language and **I can understand** a fair amount of German because my father is an Austrian, but my main language is English.

Helen: My family **speak** Aboriginal English.

Jurgen: I'**d like** Tazmann **to learn** German because part of his ancestry **is** Austrian. Me, **being** an Austrian, I **struggle to speak** the language, and **have** difficulty relating to people. I **am** an Austrian who **can't speak** his own language.

Helen: I **would love to learn to speak** the language of the Yuin, and I **would love** Tazmann **to learn** it as well, but he **won't be able to** because history **played** a role in that. Our language **was taken** away from us, stolen, gone forever, unfortunately. But he **can learn** about his culture. He **can learn** from relatives but we'**re running** out of time for that because my mother **is** pretty much the last person who **is able to share** that with him. **I guess** he **will have to learn** about it by talking to cousins, aunties, all the Aboriginal resource places he **can ever go to**, and books! If it **is ever recorded** in books, it **is** basically the only place he **can learn** about it from. Education **is** the power for the future.

Interview with Helen and Jurgen Empacher

"My name is Helen Empacher and I was born in Sydney but originally my family came from down South near Bodalla then they moved to Kempsey. The latest generation came from Kempsey I'd say, and I was born in Sydney. My mother is Aboriginal, her mother was Irish and her father was Aboriginal, and most of my family are Aboriginal. My mother is from the Yuins, I don't know a lot about them unfortunately, but I know they are from around Bodalla and that my mother being from Singleton, missed out on a lot of her culture. I found out I was a Yuin through my Mum basically, and research of my own, asking relatives and looking in books and family trees, that kind of stuff.

My father was born in Samoa with an English father and a Samoan mother but when I was younger my parents weren't together. It was basically my mother and my grandparents who raised me and I guess that Aboriginality was the identity I was given at the time. The Aboriginal part of my life was very strong it was mainly that side of my family I had a lot to do with. My father being English and having no relatives out here meant I didn't have a great deal to do with them. I guess the influence was always the Aboriginal side.

I used to say that being Aboriginal wasn't the colour of your skin it was what was in your soul. That's how I always used to describe it, and I stick to that. It's whatever is inside you, whatever experiences you've had as a kid, whatever influences you've had on your life and as they say you can take the girl out of the Aboriginal country but you can't take the Aboriginality out of the girl! I also believe even those children who had fairly light coloured skin, who were taken away from their parents and adopted, who didn't even know they were Aboriginal, still felt something within themselves that told them something wasn't quite right about their upbringing. I think they have every right to call themselves Aboriginal if they choose to identify as that later on in life, it's definitely a choice, a cultural choice.

I went to Shalvey Public School out west, my cousins went there as well so it was very much a big family thing and also the teachers took an interest in my culture I can remember it being mentioned quite a lot of times. Then I went to Sydney Girls High where I was one of the first Aboriginal students, but nothing was ever made

Interview with Helen and Jurgen Empacher

of that. I'm a primary school teacher now and in the future I would like to become more involved behind the scenes, in Aboriginal education.

Reconciliation is an important step we all need to take. We need to accept and acknowledge what has happened in the past and make amends, and our leaders need to set the example. I would like to raise my son in an open warm atmosphere full of culture and life experiences. Jurgen and I have agreed that Tazmann has to have all his cultures represented in his life so we try as much as we can to do that. Multicultural Australian means living together as one, learning to accept each other as we are, learning to accept the different cultures that now make up our country, and looking to a future where we can all work together and build a better place for our children and the future."

"My name is Jurgen Empacher and having grown up in Third World Africa with a lot of racial tension, I see Australia as one of the most ideal countries to bring up a young person in because he will be sheltered as much as possible from racial hatred and discrimination. My dream is that my son won't have to go through the same experiences that I went through. He will realise that life is not about the colour of your skin but about what you believe in.

Zimbabwe is a great country it's got a lot of culture, it's still very much alive. In the country 90% of the population still lives a very rural life and is therefore very in touch with their roots, their cultural beginnings. I would love to go back, I'd go back tomorrow if I could but economically it's not viable for me to go back with a young family, there's not a lot of hope in the economy of the country. In the future I can see myself possibly retiring in a country like Zimbabwe where life is a little more easy in some aspects, aside from the racial tension. It's got a lot more open space which is what I would like my child to have.

I think of Tazmann as an Australian, an Australian made up of Austrian, South African, Koori, Canadian, English... all mixed up. When he's older he can choose whatever he wants to be, or identify as, he's a very fitting Australian, he's a cultural melting pot himself."

Handout 2.4

Types of verbs

- **Doing** … something you **do**

I **run**	I **ran**	I **will run**

- **Thinking** … something you **think**

I **reckon**	I **guess**	I **thought**

- **Feeling** … something you **feel**

You **adore**	She **dislikes**	He **likes**

- **Saying** … something you **say**

They **whispered**	We **shouted**	I **have said**

- **Relating** … something you **are**

I **am** a woman	She **is** a chemist

… something you **have**

I **have** a sister	He **has** a wheelbarrow

The verbs below are probably **relating** verbs unless they are joined up with a **doing, feeling** or **saying** verb. Also watch for being, been, having.

To be				**To have**		
I	was	am	will be	had	have	will have
you	were	are	will be	had	have	will have
he, she, it	was	is	will be	had	has	will have
we	were	are	will be	had	have	will have
they	were	are	will be	had	have	will have

Activity Sheet 2.5

Types of Verbs

List all the different types of verbs on the activity sheet

Doing (***Action***)	**Feeling** (***Sensing***)	**Thinking** (***Sensing***)	**Saying**	**Relating** (***being or having / linking***)

Handout 2.6

Tips for Interviewing

Write down everything you need to tell the person: who you are, the purpose of the interview, what will happen afterwards, what results they can expect, etc. It is easy to forget some of this. Have your name and phone number written out to give to the person at the end of the interview.

1. Get any permissions you need (release form, etc.)
2. Start with asking some specifics: full name, maiden name, age, where the person grew up, etc.
3. Don't use closed questions, which need only a 'yes' or 'no' or similar answer, unless you want to tie them down to an admission about something.
4. Move to open ended questions after the specifics. Open ended questions should cover the information that you want in more than one way: some will be about fact (what happened then?), others will be about feelings (how did you feel when you changed jobs?), others about opinions (what do you think of? why?).
5. Prepare 'prompt' questions for important points, in case the interviewee does not give you enough information in answer to your main question. For example, if you ask: 'What did you do after school when you were my age?', have prompts ready such as 'did you play games', 'were the games different to ones today?', 'did you enjoy them?' and so on. Remember, if you don't ask the question, you won't get the information.
6. Your last question should always be something like: 'is there anything else you'd like to say about ...?' This is often when the person says the most interesting things, because they will be talking about an area you have not anticipated (if you had anticipated it, you would have included a question about it.)
7. After an interview, people often think of something they would have liked to have said but forgot. At the end of the interview, give the person your name and phone number and ask them to call you if this happens.
8. Thank them and remind them again of what will happen next and how long it will take.

Activity Sheet 2.7

Biographical Storyboard

Choose SIX significant events in the life of the interviewee and draw them or use photographs of the events. Write captions to describe the events and put them in the order in which they happened. The first picture (1) is the earliest event and (6) is the last, or most recent event.

Name:

Country of origin:

Language:

1.

2.

3.

4.

5.

6.

Model of a Biographical Recount

Stephen Raymond Seiver

Stephen Raymond Seiver grew up in a **suburb of Newcastle**, but the country he calls home runs from the North Shore of Sydney to Newcastle in the east and to the Great Dividing Range in the west. Like his grandmother who he says "was the last full blood of our tribe" Stephen is **one of the *Awabakal* people** and **that is their country**.

Stephen speaks English and some *Puli*, the language of his people. In *Puli* the name Awabakal is not used, in *Puli* the name is pronounced *Taurai*, or *Paurai*. Stephen grew up in the **1950's** and **came from a large family**, but even though he enjoyed many good times his life was harsh.

From the age of 10, when he was in 6th class at Awaba Primary School, Stephen helped his father as a timber-getter. He worked to help his family until he finished high school. **After** high school he started full time work. Stephen had some good teachers and some bad ones but he worked hard and applied himself so that he overcame all the disadvantages that he had faced at school. He **then** entered Newcastle Technical College to learn a trade. **When** he left college he worked for BHP.

Since that time Stephen has worked with electrical instruments as a technician. **Now** he is responsible for others and trains apprentices.

Stephen loves his culture which is based around the family and his country. He says his country is very beautiful, however he is worried that over-development will destroy the home of his ancestors. His **dream for the future** is that the lies about the history of his people will stop and that the truth will be told.

Activity Sheet 2.9

Biographical Recount

Title:

Orientation (When? Who? Where? Why?)

Events in time order (Use time connectives like first, then, next, while, since or dates to sequence events)

Concluding Statement

Topic 2 Multicultural Australia today

Teaching and learning activities

1. In small groups look up 'multi', 'cultural' and 'diverse'. Write a definition of all three. Explain to students that the word 'cultural' is an adjective derived from the noun 'culture'.
2. Firstly in small groups and then as a whole class discuss and develop a definition for 'multicultural Australia' or 'cultural diversity in Australia'. Ask students if they think there is any difference between the two phrases. Point out the connections between 'diverse' and 'multi' from the definitions.
3. Students list reasons why they think that Australia is a multicultural society. They should provide examples from the local community. These may include places of worship, schools, holidays, street signs, eateries and shops, festivals. Groups should report back their reasons to the class.
4. Ensure students recognise that Australia has always been 'multicultural'. Explore this idea using the following:

Focus Questions

Was everyone now living in our community born into this community? If not, where did they come from: another local community, another Australian town or city, another country? Where did members of the community's ancestors come from? Does everyone in the community share the same culture? The same language? The same beliefs and religions? How do different groups interact in our community?

---

5. Explain to students that they are going to research the diversity of experiences of people migrating to Australia currently. Display **Activity Sheet 2.10**.
6. Discuss the meanings of the headings for the areas of investigation (education, health care etc) and ask students to predict what information could be included in each area. Students should be encouraged to consider their local community as a resource.
7. Ask students what resources they might use to research this topic. Make a list of these. You may also like to add the following:

- Internet sites: **www.immi.gov.au/settle/**
  www.hreoc.gov.au
- Fiction for younger readers: *Chickpea* by Margaret Haan Syme (Scholastic 1997)
  The Sixth Worry Doll (Scholastic 1997)
  Yosou Nikki by Wendy Orr (HarperCollins 1995)
- Fiction for older readers: *Eye of the Eagle* by Ron Bunney (Fremantle Arts Centre Press 1995)
  Maddie by Brian Caswell (UQP 1995)
  Joshua by Alan Collins (UQP 1995)
  Refuge by Libby Gleeson (Penguin 1998)
  A Kind of Dreaming by Julie Ireland (HarperCollins 1995)

- Guest speaker: Local MP or city, town or shire council officer who can discuss services available to new arrivals.

8 Support students to research the information and take notes using **Activity Sheet 2.10** 'Australia – My new home'.

9 This task may be undertaken as a jigsaw activity. Students form groups of at least six members. These are called 'home groups'. Each student is then allocated a number from 1 to 6 which corresponds with the topic on **Activity Sheet 2.10**. New groups are formed of like-numbered students who are all researching the same topic – they are known as 'expert groups'. The expert groups research their topics. The home groups reform and the students share their information and new understandings with other members of the group to contribute to the final task.

10 Display and discuss the completed activity sheet. The findings could be used to contribute to a whole-class version.

11 Collect the entertainment sections of newspapers and magazines and look for articles or images that indicate Australia is a multicultural society. Tell students that 'multicultural Australia' is not only evident in the arts but is part of everyday life.

12 Display photographs of bilingual streets, shop signs, premises displaying Aboriginal flags, pamphlets and notices in a range of languages which demonstrate the wider influence of multiculturalism.

13 Make a class collage entitled 'We are Australian' which explores the image of 'an Australian'. Add captions which describe the beliefs, customs and traditions that go with the images depicted.

14 Explain that beliefs, customs and traditions are part of our families, our communities and our societies. People may have grown up with them or been introduced to them when they moved countries. Many migrants to Australia maintain aspects of their culture and religion.

15 In small groups, choose a custom, tradition or celebration that takes place in Australia to research (eg Yom Kippur, St Patrick's Day, Chinese New Year, Ramadan, Christmas). Use information already gathered as well as library resources and the Internet.

16 As a whole class write a joint construction of a factual description of one custom or celebration. Use headings and prompt questions to structure the text:

Introduction

- What is it?
- Provide other information about the origin of the custom or celebration

Characteristics

- When or why does it take place?
- What takes place?
- Who participates?

Activity Sheet 2.10

Australia – My new home

Record information about some of the problems recent migrants might face when making a new home in Australia.

1. Language

2. Accommodation

3. Health and social services

4. Employment, training and education

5. Family and friends

6. Social life (sport, entertainment, shopping)

RESOURCES

(1998) *Living languages: Warranna Puruna, Pa:mpi Tungarar – Reclamation of Aboriginal Languages.* (Video). South Australia: Department of Education, Training and Employment.

(1999) *Solid English.* Perth: Education Department of Western Australia.

(1997) *You can do it too: Aboriginal Studies and Torres Strait Islander Studies across the curriculum.* (Video). Carlton, Vic: Curriculum Corporation.

Coghill L, Ketchell J, Martin K & Price K, n.d. *Footprints ... to Country, Kin and Cultures*. Carlton, Vic: Curriculum Corporation.

Edwards V (1997) *The Other languages: A guide to multilingual classrooms*. Sydney: PETA.

Hashmi, K (1998) *You and me, Murrawee*. Ringwood, Vic: Viking.

Janeen, B (1996) *Pilawuk: When I was Young*. Flinders Park, SA: Era Publications.

Janeen, B (1996) *Maria Donato: When I was Young*. Flinders Park, SA: Era Publications.

Janeen, B (1996) *Max Colwell: When I was Young*. Flinders Park, SA: Era Publications.

Kalatzis, M and Cope B (1989) *An Overview: Teaching/learning Social Literacy*. Sydney: Common Ground.

... (1980) *Sound Literacy Series E: Connections*. Units E1-E8. Sydney: Common Ground.

... (1980) *Sound Literacy Series F: Culture* Units F1-F6. Sydney: Common Ground.

Martino W (1997) *From the margins: Exploring ethnicity, gender & Aboriginality*. Fremantle: Fremantle Arts Press.

Messenger, D R (1999) *Ceremonies and Celebrations: Vows, Tributes and Readings*. Port Melbourne: Lothian.

Pryor B & McDonald M (1999) *The Binna Binna Man*. Sydney: Allen & Unwin.

The Snowy Mountains scheme: The power of water A teacher resource guide Snowy Mountains Hydro-Electric Authority.

Understanding Australia: The Land and its People. (CD-ROM). Victoria: Department of Education.

www.hreoc.gov.au	Human Rights and Equal Opportunity Commission
www.immi.gov.au	Federal Department of Immigration and Ethnic Affairs
www.atsic.gov.au	ATSIC
www.wn.com.au/abled/	Aboriginal Education: Education Departement of Western Australia
www.acn.net.au	Australian Cultural Network (ACN)
www.dreamtime.net.au	Stories of the Dreaming (Australian Museum and ACN)
www.mov.vic.gov.au	Australian Immigration Museum

CHAPTER 3
THE ENVIRONMENT

RATIONALE

Environmental Education has the potential to ensure the well-being of future generations by promoting ecologically sustainable lifestyles. Sustainable management of the environment is one of the challenges confronting mankind. In Australia one of the most pressing environmental issues is pollution and waste management. This unit will focus on encouraging students to take positive action in preserving and managing the environment. The study of the environment will assist students to 'grow in their development as competent citizens who are prepared to play a responsible part in making our society and our world a better place.' (Social Education Association of Australia 1990). Programs need to provide experiences which focus on developing students' environmental awareness and understanding of the sustainable use and management of the environment.

Students will **identify and define the technical language** needed to talk, read and write about environmental problems and solutions. They will **research and prepare notes** on one form of recycling and **present an oral explanation of the process**. Students will be supported to use a range of temporal and causal text connectives to sequence events and **develop cause and effect relationships in an explanation**. Students will learn how to express their own views about the environment and how best to protect it. They will understand that **modal adverbs and verbs can help express forceful or tentative opinions**. This understanding of a grammatical feature will be used to support **reading and analysing text** and in **making predictions**. Students will recognise that a strong statement needs to be supported by arguments and that text connectives can be used to sequence these arguments logically in an exposition.

OVERVIEW OF SKILLS AND UNDERSTANDINGS

Studies of Society and Environment

- Identify and classify environmental issues
- Propose causes and solutions for environmental problems
- Explore recycling
- Estimate, calculate, categorise and plan
- Observe, predict, test, record and analyse water

English

- Advance a forceful argument using modal adverbs and verbs
- Write an exposition using text connectives and modal verbs and adverbs to make a forceful statement and sequence arguments and supporting reasons
- Develop information skills
- Identify and source technical language
- Explain processes orally using text connectives to indicate time and cause

TOPICS

Content	Sample Teaching and Learning Activities	Skills – Studies of Society and Environment	Skills – English
Topic 1 Issues in our cities and towns			
Suggestions of causes of observed environmental problems: air pollution, water pollution, waste disposal, population, and urban development. Suggestions of possible solutions.	Identify local and national environmental problems and potential causes. Respond to environmental problems with solutions, using the 'will it?' test, including locally.	Reading and talking about visual cues. Making an individual, sensory and emotional response. Proposing solutions, testing proposed solutions and discussing possible multiple solutions.	Examining and discussing visual cues and details. Advancing a forceful argument using modal adverbs and verbs. Predicting responses. Writing an exposition.
Topic 2 Let's recycle!			
Investigations into waste disposal and recycling in a school community. Exploration of the stages and processes of recycling. Understanding reusable and disposable materials.	Investigate and develop knowledge and understandings about recycling processes.	Weighing, estimating, calculating, categorising, locating and planning for improvement. Exploring models of recycling. Identifying reusable and recyclable products in common use.	Developing information skills. Defining technical language. Explaining orally using text connectives / conjunctions to indicate time and cause. Use text connectives in an oral explanation.

Topic 1 Issues in our cities and towns

Teaching and learning activities

1 Display **Handout 3.1**. In pairs, get students to discuss what's happening in the illustration.

2 As a whole class, have students brainstorm all the problems they can see.

3 Write each example on a flash card and using a large wall chart, have students classify the problems in columns under the following headings:

- people
- other creatures
- plants and the land
- the water
- the air

4 Ask students to imagine they are in the picture in **Handout 3.1**. In pairs have them explain how it feels. These questions may help as prompts for their responses.

Focus Questions

Listen to all the noises of cars, trucks, buses, planes, motorbikes. How does the noise make you feel?

Taste the water. What is it like?

Smell the air. Is it fresh?

Look at the sky. What colour(s) is it?

---

5 Ask students to focus on the characters in the illustration in **Handout 3.1** and to discuss what they may be saying. Have students write down these comments in speech bubbles which can be added to the picture. Make sure students know who they are talking to. Model one and then let students work in pairs and add others.

6 **Activity Sheet 3.2** provides a range of environmental solutions. Using the 'will it?' questions on the Handout, model the thinking and questioning process. Then have students working individually on evaluating the solutions presented.

7 In pairs, students can discuss their favoured solutions giving reasons for their choices, against the 'Will it' questions.

8 Ask each student to select one of the environmental problems in the illustration or included in **Activity Sheet 3.2** and their most favoured solution(s). This will be the basis for their written exposition.

9 Explain to students that one of the ways we often express tentativeness or certainty about something in English is by using a *modal verb*, or *adverb* or a subjective or objective expression. Model some of the language by firstly using examples students are familiar with (eg, Popeye **must** eat his spinach if he wants to be strong. The Broncos **should** beat the Eels but **there's no doubt** the Bulldogs will win the Grand Final.).

⑩ Make up sets of cards from **Handout 3.3** using a different colour for *verbs*, for *adverbs* and for subjective/objective expressions. Make enough sets to allow students to work in small groups. (If the grammatical categories are designated by colour, the cards can be used in other activities to show how verbal groups can be built up using adverbs and modal verbs eg. "That film *will probably run* for a few months.")

⑪ In small groups let students sort the *modal verbs*, *modal adverbs*, and subjective/objective expressions. They should place the cards under three headings: *forceful, medium* and *tentative*. Many students, especially bilingual students, may find difficulty with these words. Although they are frequently used in oral language, they are not often explicitly taught, and can be confusing.

⑫ After sorting them ask students to put all the cards of the same colour next to each other in each column. Distribute **Handout 3.3** so they can check their classifications with the mastercopy.

⑬ Using a wall chart of **Handout 3.3** to assist them, ask students to prepare a 30 second speech using *forceful* language to express their opinions about their selected environmental problem/solution.

⑭ Highlight some of the *forceful* language that students use in their 30 second oral presentations.

⑮ Students can consider different problems and suggest probable causes by completing **Activity Sheet 3.4**. Before attempting to finish the sentences, have them read the stems of the answers aloud and check the wall chart to predict if their answers will be *forceful, medium* or *tentative.*

⑯ In small groups, ask students to role play an interview by a radio, TV or newspaper reporter with people stuck in city traffic and then present it to the class. Remind students to use *modal adverbs*, *verbs* or an expression to help express the strength of their character's opinions.

⑰ Students can then use their notes and the scaffold in **Activity Sheet 3.5** to develop arguments for an exposition on the topic 'Our cities – what's wrong?'

⑱ In a joint construction or individually, you can guide students in writing the exposition. Prompt them to make notes about

- the problem(s) being experienced
- the feelings these problems arouse
- their possible solutions

Remind the class to use *modal adverbs*, *verbs* or objective/subjective expressions to help them express the strength and conviction of their arguments.

⑲ The collection of final expositions could be published together as a class book or compiled and sent to a local member or the Minister for the Environment.

Our Cities and Towns

Activity Sheet 3.2

Solutions to problems in our cities and towns

This sheet refers to the illustration in Handout 3.1 and can also be adapted to suit your local context.

Thinking time

WILL IT … fix the problem? … help with part of the problem? … be likely that people will try it?

WILL IT … cost me or someone money? … take time? … have much chance of working?

WILL IT … cost us some freedom? … cost us in other ways, for example, convenience?

WILL IT … save energy? … use materials and resources wisely? … help the environment?

WILL IT … help us be more healthy? … help people to have jobs? … help other creatures?

WILL IT … be good for the future? … be too far-fetched? … be practical?

WILL IT … be able to start tomorrow? … make us happier?

On this page and the next are several problems and a list of possible solutions for each one. Use the thinking suggestions to help solve the problems. Place number **1**, **2** or **3** in the brackets for your choice of best solutions. (**1** = Excellent solution, **2** = Very good solution, and **3** = Good solution)

Remember to use the WILL IT tests.

We can clean the air up if …

We ban all private cars ( )

We improve public transport and use it more ( )

We work more from home ( )

We allow car use only on some days ( )

We make petrol very expensive ( )

We all walk to school or to work ( )

Activity Sheet 3.2 (continued)

Solutions to problems in our cities and towns

We make fewer car trips ( )
We fine drivers heavily if their exhausts pollute the air ( )
We share cars more ( )
We go back to using more horse-drawn vehicles ( )

We can reduce pollution from fossil fuels (coal, oil, natural gas) if...

We close all factories ( )
We put factories/power stations where winds blow smoke away ( )
We filter all chimneys ( )
We make all electricity from solar, wind and water power ( )
We fine factories and power stations ( )
We allow only essential lighting and appliances that emit smoke ( )
We use lots of money to develop other kinds of energy ( )
We have all factories, separated, a long way from cities ( )
We use fewer factory-made products ( )
We recycle as many materials as we can ( )

We can best help creatures and the natural environment if...

We ban production of all greenhouse gases ( )
We use only natural, not manufactured, materials ( )
We plant trees and shrubs in every place we can ( )
We set up huge conservation areas far away from cities ( )
We recycle as many materials as we can ( )
We let nature look after itself ( )
We ask each person to act responsibly ( )
We penalise people who harm the environment ( )
We dispose of all waste far out at sea ( )
We get rid of all introduced plants and creatures ( )

Reproduced from (1998) NRMA Clean Air 2000 Kit

Handout 3.3

Degrees of Certainty

One of the ways we often express tentativeness or certainty about something in English is by using a modal verb, or adverb or an expression eg "You **might** like to recycle. You **must** recycle. I will **probably** recycle. **I'm adamant that** we must reduce, reuse and recycle".

Forceful	Medium	Tentative
Modal Verbs		
must has to, have to should ought	will may	might could would can can't
Modal Adverbs		
certainly for sure surely no doubt undoubtedly without fail definitely absolutely	probably presumably arguably	possibly perhaps maybe
Subjective and objective expressions		
Subjective		
I know I'm sure I bet I'm adamant that	I guess I should think I think I don't think I reckon I suppose I don't believe I bet	I doubt I suspect
Objective		
it's certain there's no doubt there's no way it's obvious	it's probable it seems likely it's unlikely it's likely it appears that	it's possible there's a possibility there's a chance

(see Derewianka 1998: 66)

Activity Sheet 3.4

Cause and effect

Consider different problems and suggest probable causes.

Why is it hard to see the bridge? It could be because …

Why are there so many cars end to end? Maybe …

Why are those people wearing masks? I think …

How could you cut down the number of cars? I suppose …

How did the water get so dirty that you can't swim? If …

What can we do about the trees? We need to …

Those factory chimneys put out loads of smoke. Maybe that's because …

What's making everyone look so angry? I'm sure …

Why aren't people taking notice of the warning? I reckon …

Activity Sheet 3.5

Exposition

Topic:

Main argument (say what you think about the topic – use a modal verb or adverb like "should" or "definitely" to express how strongly you feel)

Arguments (use connectives such as firstly, secondly, thirdly to put your arguments in order. Support each argument with a reason)

Firstly …

Secondly …

Thirdly …

Summarise your main argument (use a connective like "as a result", "as a consequence", "therefore" to begin your summary)

Topic 2 Let's recycle!

Teaching and learning activities

1. Explain that recycling means to use resources over and over again and is about conserving our resources and saving energy. Have the whole class brainstorm meanings for all technical terms related to the topic of recycling, ie 'carbon dioxide, fine particle pollution, raw materials, dissolve, sink, suspend, substance, purify'.

2. In small groups, ask students to look up all the terms in the dictionary or encyclopaedia to provide exact definitions and try to find one with a similar meaning in the thesaurus.

3. Compile all the groups' definitions and synonyms in a class chart to scaffold students' vocabulary for this topic.

4. To provide an understanding of the extent of waste disposal, begin with your school environment. Estimate at the beginning of the week how much waste is created in one day and over longer periods. Gather and sort waste created by the class in one day and over a week. Compare the actual results at the end of the week with the class estimates (**Activity Sheet 3.6**). Use a standard measure (eg a bucket or garbage bin).

5. Having collected the waste over a week, have the students spread the waste in an area in the playground. Using gloves, suggest that they sort and classify the waste materials according to type and material (eg food, paper, glass, plastic, aluminium).

6. Students can make a class chart showing how much was in each category. Also include a place on the chart for 'sources' and 'solutions' for each category of waste.

7. Hold a class discussion focusing on where the waste comes from: food, packaging, home, school etc. Add these to the sources column on the class chart.

8. Brainstorm different ways of reducing the amount of waste. Add this information to the chart.

9. Let students use the information about water pollution to create a diagram using **Activity Sheet 3.7**. Create a diagram of the journey of pollutants which are being flushed into the sea. Label these boxes and draw pictures in them to show what is happening then connect them with arrows. In the last box which is labelled for you, show what the water looks like and what is floating in it when it finally flows into the sea.

10. Gather clean, transparent jars and fill them 3/4 full with clean water. Have students add a spoonful of the following substances (cereal, soil, washing powder, vegetable dye, oil, other). The grid in **Activity Sheet 3.8** can be used to predict, observe and record their findings.

11. As a whole class brainstorm the effects on health for

   - plants
   - animals
   - fish
   - humans

   if they use water containing any or all of these substances. Record these on a large mind map.

12. In small groups, investigate the recycling of plastics, glass, paper or any other product that can be recycled, for a short class presentation. Ideas for research might include kits and videos provided by commercial companies such as Comalco, ACI, Australian Paper; an excursion to a recycling or waste plant; and interview with local city or shire council officers responsible for recycling. Students may use the chart **Activity Sheet 3.9** to help collect and classify information.

13. Explain to students that words which contribute to the cohesion of the text are called *text connectives*. They provide a reader with signposts showing how the text is developing. They may be used to show the relationship between *cause* and a *result*. Give out **Handout 3.10** to assist groups with their oral presentations.

14. Each group should nominate a reporter who will present an oral explanation to the class. Remind the reporter to use some *text connectives* as shown in **Handout 3.10** to sequence the explanation.

Class or School Waste Record

Estimate for 1 day	Estimate for 1 week	Estimate for 1 month	Estimate for 1 year
Actual Containers for 1 day	**Actual Containers for 1 week**	**Actual Containers for 1 month**	**Actual Containers for 1 year**

Did you know that …

every person in a large city produces approximately 400kg of household waste a year. For every person another 400kg of industrial waste is produced per year. Combined this means that nearly the equivalent of 1 tonne of waste is produced for every person. This is equivalent to the weight of a small car.

Activity Sheet 3.7

Water Pollution

Lots of paving in cities and suburbs means that when it rains more water rushes faster into drains before the earth can soak it up. If stormwater overflows it can wash untreated sewage into the sea. Any mess left on roads or footpaths like oils, chemicals, rubbish and animal waste is also washed into the sea. Create a diagram which shows the cause and effects of pollutants being flushed in to the sea. Consider the waste items you found in the school environment and others that would be caught in drains, left on roads and footpaths. Draw what's happening and write a caption to the right of the box.

Stormwater run-off flowing into the sea.

Activity Sheet 3.8

Water Pollution Experiment

You will need at least six clean, transparent jars.

1. Fill them 3/4 full with clean water.
2. Predict what will happen when each substance is added.
3. Add a spoonful of the substances shown in the grid.
4. Record what you see immediately, when the jar is shaken and after a short time.

Substance	Predict: what will happen when substance is added to water?	Observe: is it dissolved, does it sink, is it suspended?	Record: what happens if stirred, shaken?	Record: what happens if left to stand?	Other comments
Cereal					
Soil					
Washing powder					
Vegetable dye					
Oil					
Other					

Activity Sheet 3.9

Collection, sorting and making new products

Fill in the rubbish or waste product your group is researching. Then answer the questions.

Recycling ☐ plastic ☐ paper ☐ glass ☐ aluminium ☐ food ☐ cardboard	
Collection of ________________ rubbish for recycling • How is it collected? • Who collects it? • What happens to it?	
Sorting ____________________ • Why does it have to be sorted? • How is it sorted? • What happens to it after it is sorted?	
Making new products from ____________________ • What new product can be made? • What are the steps in this process?	

Handout 3.10

Text Connectives

Words which contribute to the cohesion of the text are called text connectives and/or conjunctions. They provide the reader with signposts which show how the text is developing. They may be used to show the relationship between a cause and a result.

Showing cause/result	Indicating time
so	then
therefore	next
then	afterwards
consequently	at the same time
in/as a consequence	before that
as a result	in the end
for that reason	finally
due to…, owing to…	soon
accordingly	after a while
because of this	at this point
in that case	meanwhile
	at this moment
	later
	previously
	earlier
	until then

(Derewianka 1998: 110)

RESOURCES

(1998) *Geography for Primary Schools*. South Australia: Department of Education, Training and Employment.

(1998) National Curriculum Services *Clean Air 2000*. Sydney: NRMA.

(1990) *Social Education in the Nineties: A Basic Right for Every Person.* Sydney: Social Education Association of Australia).

(1998) *Sustaining Environemental Education*. South Australia: Department of Education, Training and Employment.

Suzuki, D (1999) *You are the Earth*. Sydney: Allen & Unwin.

www.greeningaustralia.org.au/	Greening Australia
www.peg.apc.org/~twsnat/	The Wilderness Society
www.planetark.org/	Planet Ark
www.sofcom.com.au/Greenpeace	Greenpeace
www.erin.gov.au/	Environment Australia Online
www.csiro.doe.gov	Sustainable Development
www.landcarensw.org.au	Landcare
www.cleanup.com.au	Clean Up Australia

CHAPTER 4
THEN AND NOW

RATIONALE

'Time, continuity and change' is an area in Studies of Society and Environment which requires students to carry out historical inquiry. Students gain a richer understanding of cultural, historical, environmental and technological change by comparing the past and present and are able to develop insights into our possible future. This area of study also provides opportunities for students to investigate aspects of the local area by using primary and secondary sources; learning about natural, heritage and built features in the local area, and other communities in Australia; and, identifying causes and effects of change in communities. Information can be acquired from a range of sources, eg newspapers, CD-ROMs, Internet, books, oral histories, photographic images and museum exhibits.

Students will become **aware of appropriate grammatical, oral and written choices** that can be made when discussing history and social change. Students will **discuss the past and present using adjectives, comparatives and superlatives** to compare the differences between *then* and *now*. Students will **make oral comparisons** and **write a discussion** about one aspect of life that has changed. They will **identify and use adverbs and adverbial phrases** to give information about when, where, how and in what way, events occur.

OVERVIEW OF SKILLS AND UNDERSTANDINGS

Studies of Society and Environment

- Research changes in society
- Identify, classify and discuss change
- Describe and compare changes
- Explain a point of view
- Predict change

English

- Use adjectives, comparatives and superlatives
- Make comparisons orally
- Use adverbs and adverbial phrases to give information about when, where, how and in what way, events occur
- Write a discussion

TOPICS

Content	Sample Teaching and Learning Activities	Skills – Studies of Society and Environment	Skills – English
Topic 1 Our community – Then and now			
Newspaper images of our local community then and now.	Gather and compare newspaper images of the local area. Identify significant changes in the local area. Predict future changes.	Researching using local newspapers. Comparing, identifying, classifying and discussing change in the local area.	Using comparative adjectives. Making comparisons.
Topic 2 Transport – Then and now			
Changes to transport in the last century in Australia.	Research changes in transport in the last 100 years. Discuss the relationship between technology and change.	Researching, discussing, analysing, evaluating and writing about the history of transport in the last century in Australia.	Using adverbs and adverbial phrases of place, time manner and accompaniment. Writing a discussion.

Topic 1 Our community – Then and now

Teaching and learning activities

1. Explain that a newspaper is an everyday text with multiple purposes and readers; it not only informs but also educates and entertains the reader. Ask students to help you collect local newspapers and magazines, especially old ones which might be lining cupboards or stored away.

2. Have students cut out things which can be used to illustrate 'then' and 'now'. Things to look for could be examples of

   - advertisements (either the product or the way it is advertised have changed)
   - editorials which discuss some social or political change (eg the law to give equal pay to women, or include Aboriginal Australians in the census)
   - features (showing changes in attitudes or social behaviour)
   - cartoons (showing changes in attitudes or social behaviour)
   - news articles (reports about places, buildings, social change)

3. Create a class display under the headings 'Then' and 'Now' and add a caption to each picture, or a summary of each article, that gives details of the differences eg.

   Food

   In the past many people ate a lot of meat products and fats.

   Now more people eat healthier food and food from countries such as China and Thailand.

   Equal pay for women

   Once women were paid less than men for doing the same job.

   More recently, women and men are paid the same amount of money if they do the same job.

4. Focus on ONE or more of the areas below that is appropriate to your local community and ask students to brainstorm ideas about what things were like 'then' and what they are like 'now'. Use **Activity Sheet 4.1**.

   - families
   - buildings
   - clothing
   - school and education
   - environment
   - housing
   - work
   - technology
   - shopping

   If you are looking at a local building or area, consider a visit to a local museum, tourist information centre, historical society, building of significance etc to explore 'then' further. On their return to the classroom, students can then brainstorm what the building or area is like 'now'.

5. As a whole class, formulate a list of questions to find out more about one or more of the topic above in your city or town. From this list identify what key questions students could ask a local adult. For example,

---

Focus Questions

What things have changed at home/school/town centre/in technology/at work since you were a child? What do you think of these changes? Are they for the better? Why do you think this? Can you think of something that has changed that you are not happy about?

---

6. Ask students to pair up. This will allow them to take different responsibilities for organising, conducting and reporting the interview. Remind students that the focus for the topic and the interview are the differences between 'then' and 'now' in the community. As students will be reporting back to each other, each pair could focus on a different topic for comparison, ie families, school and education, work, buildings, environment, technology, clothing, housing, etc.

7. Assist students to locate and identify local people to interview. Refer to **Handout 2.6** in Chapter 2 for tips on interviewing.

8. Explain to students that *adjectives* play a significant role in building information around *nouns*. Adjectives can give information about

   - quantity (one, half a dozen, many)
   - facts/attributes (small, red, dark)
   - value/attributes (beautiful, odd, funny)
   - type/classification (American, oceanic)
   - comparisons (kindest, older, angrier, more difficult, fatter, more run down)

   (Derewianka 1998: 30)

9. Display the **Handout 4.2** to support students to use *adjectives* when describing and making comparisons. Ask students to try to guess their interviewee's opinions by using the sentences with blanks and putting in their own *adjectives, comparatives* or *superlatives*.

10. Ask each student to give an oral report of their interview. They should say who they interviewed, who they are and about what topic (eg "I interviewed *Mr Jeff Campbell*. He is the *Lord Mayor*. I asked him about *school* 'then and now'"). Ask students to use comparison *adjectives* when they present their report to the whole class (eg "Mr Campbell said that schools were *stricter* then. He also said that schools today have *more technology* and *larger classes*".

11. Students can choose the topic they have been working on, or another one from the list in Activity 3. Choose one example from the list to model for the class. Ask students to suggest what changes they think could occur in the future. Write the focus question up and ask students to make predictions for their topic.

Focus Questions

What is it like now? Is it likely to change? In what ways will it be different? (faster, healthier, larger, more polluted, friendlier, more difficult).

---

12. Have students draw a diagram or illustration to show their predictions. Ask them to label the diagram or write captions under pictures, to show what the changes are (improvements or damages).

Activity Sheet 4.1

Brainstorm – Then and Now

Topic:

Then:

Now:

Handout 4.2

Using Comparative Adjectives

Here are some adjectives to help you compare 'then' and 'now'.

1. Some adjectives have a completely different form when you use them to compare, eg good/better/best

   The Eagles are **bad** but the Sharks are **worse** and the Tigers are the **worst** team.
   Adjective *Comparative* *Superlative*

2. But most just add ..**er** or .. **est**, eg kind/ kinder/ kindest

   She is **kind** to everyone but even **kinder** to her friends and she is **kindest** to her family.
   Adjective *Comparative* *Superlative*

3. Longer words, with more than two syllabus do not change – just add another word

   Sydney is **beautiful** but Adelaide is **more** beautiful and Perth is the **most** beautiful city of all.

   Private cars cause the **most** pollution but travel by bus causes **less** pollution and travel by train causes the **least**.

Then it was ______________________________ than now.

eg **quieter**
less polluted
easier

Then families were ______________________________ than now.

Then school was ______________________________ than now.

Then jobs were ______________________________ than now.

Then cars were ______________________________ than now.

Then buildings were ______________________________ than now.

Then the environment was ______________________________ than now.

Now it is ______________________________ than then.

eg **noisier**
more polluted
harder

Now families are ______________________________ than then.

Now school is ______________________________ than then.

Now jobs are ______________________________ than then.

Now cars are ______________________________ than then.

Now buildings are ______________________________ than then.

Now the environment is ______________________________ than then.

Topic 2 Transport – Then and now

Teaching and learning activities

1. Divide the class into THREE small groups. Each group will research an area of transport: choose train, sea or air travel. This research will form the basis of a discussion about 'Transport – Then and now'.

2. Give out **Handout 4.3** to introduce the topics. Write up a timeline beginning in 1850 and finishing in the present day. Mark on it when these events took place. As students research the history of transport in Australia and elsewhere they will be able to add to the timeline.

3. **Activity Sheet 4.4** can be used to guide students researching in the library or on the Internet. Before they research travel in the past 100 years, they can begin to fill in the right-hand column (Transport Now) based on what they currently know. Ask them to focus on comfort, dangers and safety, speed and reliability, technology.

Focus Questions

What comforts can passengers expect? What does the transport look like inside and out? What dangers do travellers face? What safety measures are taken to protect passengers? How long do journeys take? Are there many breakdowns or delays? Why? What power source is used? Are many people needed to run the transport? Is the transport environmentally friendly?

---

4. Have students form pairs to explore some of the differences between an automobile today and one earlier last century. Use the web site **http://www.pwaf.com.au/veteran/history/contents.html**, car magazines, newspapers liftouts.

5. Hand out **Activity Sheet 4.5**. Explain that each pair needs to choose two specific car makes and models from different years between 1900–1950 and 1950–2000. Ask them to record the details in the columns. They can also draw the two cars, labelling the differences or improvements.

6. Explain to students that *abverbials* are words and phrases that provide extra detail about what is happening. They answer the questions Where? Why? How? With whom? Using what? For how long? Display examples of *adverbials* in the classroom and highlight the relationship between the *adverb* or *adverbial phrase* and how it gives information about when, where and how an action takes place.

7. To introduce students to *adverbs* and *adverbial phrases* play the adverbials game. Using **Handout 4.6**, make three posters of *adverbials How? Where? When?* for the classroom. Display the list of *action verbs* and make a set of cards to match them. These are stacked face down. A student chooses a card with an *action verb* on it and does not show anyone. Using any of the *adverbials* from the list (and others you may add), the rest of the class ask questions in turn to deduce what *action verb* the student is holding, eg Do you do it in the morning? Do you do it with a friendly smile? Do you do it at your desk?

8 Using the structure and prompts on **Activity Sheet 4.7** to explain to students that a discussion states the case both 'for' and 'against' an idea or statement. These statements could be anything which expresses a point of view: 'We need to preserve Australia's rainforests'; 'Australia should become a republic', 'Children have more fun that adults'. Both 'sides' of the discussion need to be supported by arguments, reasons and examples.

9 Explain to students that they are to write a discussion about transport 'then' and 'now'. They can choose to write about the two cars researched in Activity 5, or any other aspect of transport using the statement 'Then is better than now'. Students could compare and contrast driving the cars 'then' and 'now' and include things like cost to buy, cost to run and repair, speed, safety, reliability, comfort, appearance, environmental impact. If writing about air, sea and rail travel they can use their notes from **Activity Sheet 4.4**.

10 Students will need support using

- *connectives* (such as: first, then, next, finally to sequence arguments) when posing the arguments for 'then'
- *adverbials* to give information about where, when and how actions occur for 'now'
- *adjectives, comparatives* and *superlatives* to make comparisons and conclusions in the conclusion (see **Handout 4.2**)

Travel tales

Train travel

In 1884 on the 2nd of April, two trains collided at Werribee, Victoria killing three people. By the turn of the century Australians were not strangers to train travel but it was of a very different kind to that enjoyed by train travellers today.

Sea Travel

In 1900 when the SS Glenelg sank killing 31 people, there was a public outcry. Evidence heard from seamen included claims that the ship's crankshaft was cracked and that plates which covered holes in the hull were only one sixteenth of an inch thick. Passenger and cargo ships sinking around the turn of the century was quite common.

Air travel

In 1935, Sir Charles Kingsford-Smith went missing when flying a small aeroplane. Lady Kingsford-Smith said that she was confident that her husband had landed in an isolated spot and was unable to establish communication with the outside world, Kingsford-Smith was never seen again. It was not the first time he had been reported missing and he was not the first aviator to die flying. Charles Ulm the man who flew with Smith on many occasions went down in his plane the year before and Amelia Earhart disappeared during her around-the-world flight two years later.

Activity Sheet 4.4

Differences between then and now

________________ Travel in the last 100 years in Australia.

THEN	NOW
Comfort:	**Comfort:**
Dangers and safety:	**Dangers and safety:**
Speed and reliability:	**Speed and reliability:**
Technology:	**Technology:**

Activity Sheet 4.5

History of Cars

In 1910 the Ford Motor Company had a successful first year selling 400 cars. In 1917 Holden Co South Australia started building motor car bodies.

Refer to web site: Automobile History **http://www.pwaf.com.au/veteran/history/contents.html**

THEN 1900-1950	**NOW 1950-2000**
Make:	**Make:**
Model:	**Model:**
Year:	**Year:**
Special Features:	**Special Features:**

Handout 4.6

The Adverbial Game

Action Verbs	How?	Where?	When?
smile	with a friendly …	outside	in the morning
sleep	quietly	at my desk	at lunchtime
read	fast	in the car	at weekends
sit	very quickly	in the kitchen	after school
write	politely	at school	before school
read	very well	in a car	during lunch
eat	happily	in a tree	
scream	with fear	in an airplane	
run	thankfully	in my bedroom	
jump		in the playground	
dance			
play			
fly			
fall			
skip			
breathe			
travel			

Activity Sheet 4.7

Discussion

Topic: ***"Then is better than now."***

State the case 'for' and support with reasons (use connectives such as: first, then, next, finally to sequence arguments)

State the case "against" and support with reasons (use adverbials to give information about where, when and how actions occur)

Conclusion (use adjectives, comparatives and superlatives to make comparisons)

RESOURCES

(1999) *Look Inside Cross sections: Ships*. Ringwood, Vic: Penguin.

(1995) *Look Inside Cross sections: Cars*. Ringwood, Vic: Penguin.

(1995) *Look Inside Cross sections: Trains*. Ringwood, Vic: Penguin.

(1994) *Look Inside Cross sections: Planes*. Ringwood, Vic: Penguin.

www.aa.gov.au/AA_WWW/AA_home_Page.html	Australian Archives
www.anmm.gov.au	Australian Maritime Museum
www.questacon.edu.au	Questacon: The National Science and Technology Centre
www.dca.gov.au/oph.html	Old Parliament House
www.phm.gov.au	Powerhouse Museum
http://users.wantree.com.au/~ramjet/arhs/museum/musframe.htm	Rail Transport Museum

CHAPTER 5
AUSTRALIA AS PART OF THE GLOBAL VILLAGE

RATIONALE

The purpose of global education is to help students to develop into active global citizens. It helps to develop the skills, knowledge and attitudes which young people will need to participate in the process of local and global change which will ensure the well-being of our world. Global education promotes a cross-curricula approach so students can understand what can make 'the far away' 'closer to home' and see that local events and actions can have global implications. Students can learn practical skills so that they are able to participate in the shaping of their future world. They should develop understandings about the values of global solidarity, peace and tolerance.

Students will **critically read and view texts** and **locate and select specific information**. They will be supported to **use a range of everyday texts and media resources**, and to develop skills and strategies **to skim and scan for specific information**. The ability **to identify and write topic sentences** will be developed and used to support **reading to locate information**, and **to organise writing into paragraphs**. A focus on the theme of the topic sentence will support students **to develop complex sentences**.

OVERVIEW OF SKILLS AND UNDERSTANDINGS

Studies of Society and Environment

- Gather and organise information
- Cooperate in groups
- Reflect on relationships between individuals and communities
- Draw conclusions based on given facts

English

- Critically read and view a range of media and everyday texts
- Locate and select specific information – skim and scan
- Identify and write topic sentences
- Write an explanation

TOPICS

Content	Sample Teaching and Learning Activities	Skills – Studies of Society and Environment	Skills – English
Topic 1 What is global aid?			
Learning about the work of global aid workers.	Investigate global aid to gain knowledge of countries, projects, needs and aid workers' skills.	Gathering, organising, recording and reporting information. Working cooperatively in a team. Developing the ability to reflect.	Identifying topic sentences. Scanning for specific information in everyday texts by looking at topic sentences.
Topic 2 Working together – How can we help?			
Community needs and reflecting on aid responses. (*Global Education Resource* video)	View video section 6 *Bridging Co-operation: Helping people help themselves* and last section 'Environment and development'. Consider community needs and agencies' work. Reflect on individual roles in making a difference to the state of the world.	Developing critical literacy and viewing skills. Reflecting, analysing and drawing conclusions.	Writing topic sentences. Organising writing into paragraphs. Writing an explanation.

Topic 1 What is global aid?

Teaching and learning activities

❶ Introduce the topic of global aid with **Handout 5.1**, the advertisement 'Wanted: A global aid worker'. Point out to students the context and purpose of this text.

Focus Questions

What do you think a global aid worker does? What kind of person would make a good aid worker? Does anyone know an aid worker?

---

❷ Have students look at the advertisements in **Handout 5.3**. They should then attempt to complete the first column 'What we knew at the start' on **Activity Sheet 5.4**.

❸ Ask students in pairs, to research ONE of the following topics using library resources, current newspapers, magazines and the Internet.

Topic Questions

What is relief work? What is development work? What is a disaster? What are some examples of disaster work? What are human rights? What is a refugee? How do global workers help refugees? What is a developing country? Where are some developing countries?

---

❹ Brainstorm a list of Key Words to look for. These can be used by students to define, locate, and select information from library catalogues, book indexes, through search engines (eg Yahoo, Alta Vista) on the Internet or inside a text.

❺ Encourage students to take notes using bullet points and to be as brief as possible, recording key words or phrases, just enough to convey meaning. Provide the following headings for students

- Date
- Research topic
- Text (ie video, book, website, pamphlet)
- Title
- Author
- Key words to look for
- Main ideas

❻ Ask students to form pairs. Give each pair a newspaper and a highlighter pen. Ask them to *skim* through the newspaper and look for articles relevant to the topic questions in Activity 3 by looking at the following features of articles:

- Headlines
- Subheadings
- Bold print
- Photographs
- Diagrams
- Charts
- Illustration captions
- Graphs
- Cartoons

7. When students have selected what they think might be a relevant newspaper article, ask them to highlight the first sentence and/or *topic sentence* in each paragraph. They should then read the highlighted text. If it is clear from this text that the article is relevant to the topics, they can then *scan* for specific information by looking at topic sentences and highlighting them.

8. Using **Activity Sheet 5.2**, develop a whole class concept map on 'What is global aid?'. Students can use their research notes and the newspaper articles they have collected to contribute.

9. Ask students to brainstorm cooperative skills, and how to share responsibility when working on a group task. Begin by asking them to reflect on the problems and successes of working in pairs to find the newspaper article. Ask them to predict what will happen working in larger groups.

10. In groups of 4, have students work as a team to research and complete the second column of **Activity Sheet 5.4** 'What we found out after research'. In addition to using the Internet and newspapers, students should be encouraged to contact aid organisations such as UNICEF, World Vision, Community Aid Abroad, Austcare and Amnesty International and ask for further information in the form of brochures, pamphlets and magazines which may be produced by the organisations.

11. Using the multiple pages of **Handout 5.5**, allow each team choose ONE of the UNICEF Australia Projects 1992–93 and produce an oral presentation for the class which includes:

    - locating the country on a world map
    - giving a summary of the UNICEF project
    - noting any new information on the role of the aid worker
    - stating the roles and responsibilities each team member assumed in preparing the presentation

    The team should all support the presentation, although their roles might not include speaking in the presentation.

12. Following the teams' presentations to the whole class, add any new information from their reports to the class concept map 'What is global aid?'.

Handout 5.1

'Wanted: A global aid worker!'

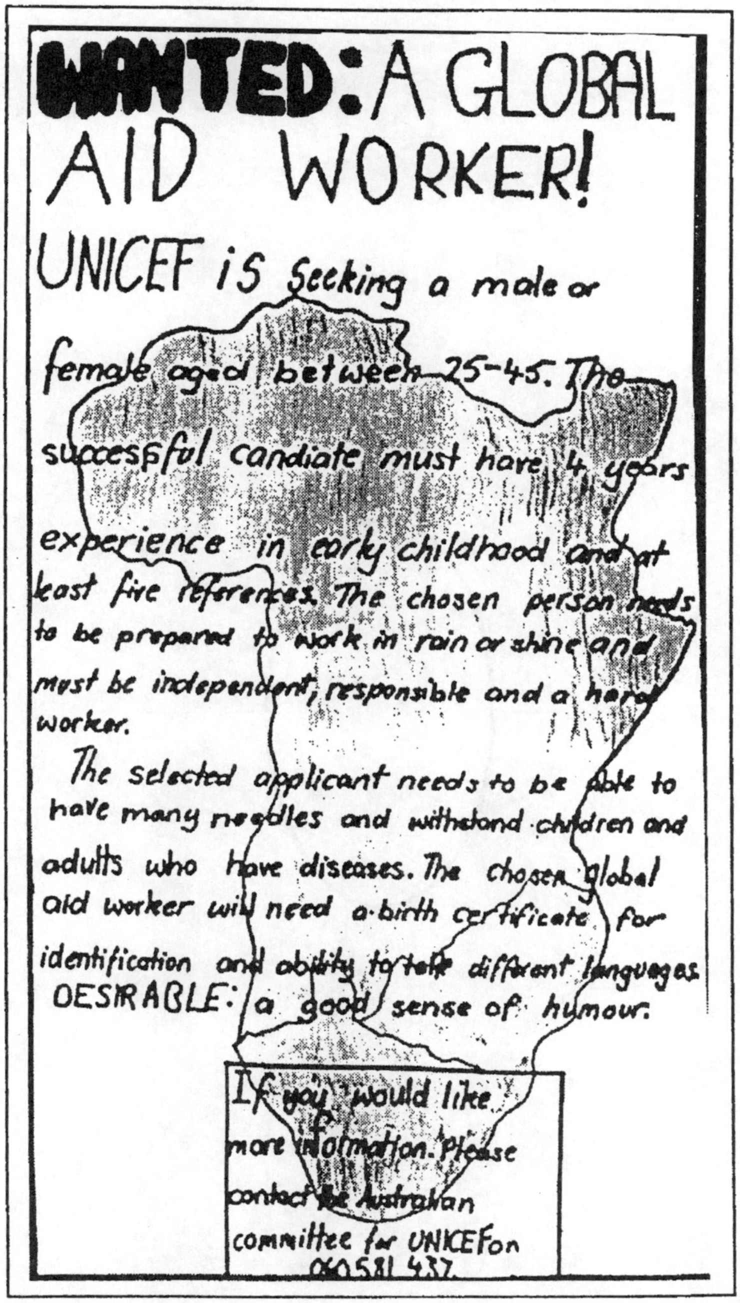

(1996) Global Education Resource

Activity Sheet 5.2

Concept Map

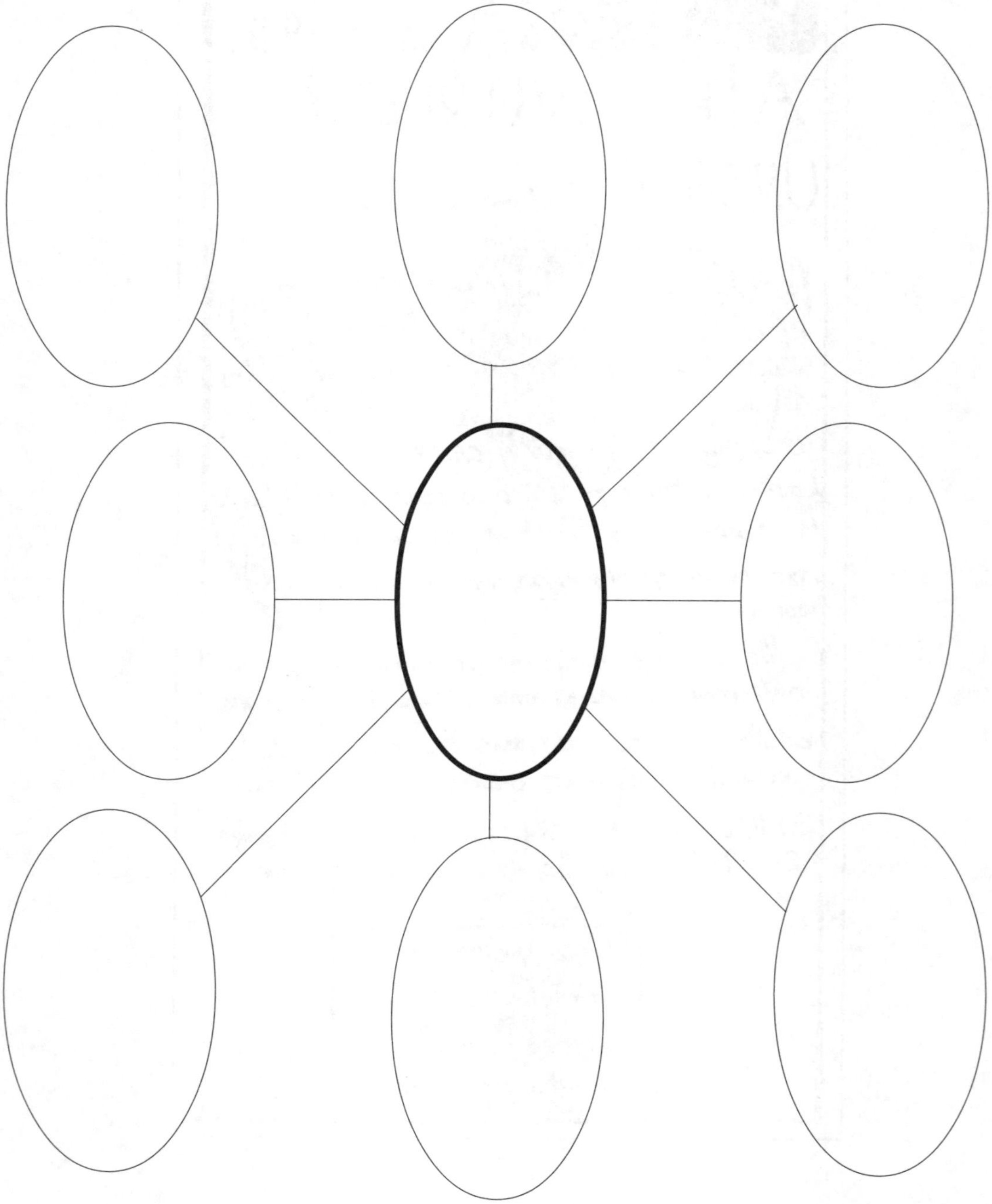

'Wanted: A global aid worker!' Actual Advertisements

AusAID

Wanted: Global Aid Worker

People with experience in planning and managing development education projects are invited to submit proposals under AusAID's Development Education Program in Special Projects.

Priority areas:

- trade and development issues
- Papua New Guinea and/or the Pacific.

For details please contact:

AusAID

GPO Box 887
Canberra City 2601

unicef
AUSTRALIA

Wanted: Global Aid Worker

This challenging and rewarding position requires a mature person with knowledge of both relief and development work in the Third World. Field experience in a specialised area is essential. The successful candidate will be expected to have an understanding of, and commitment to, improving living conditions of the poor of both North and South as well as a sound understanding of disaster work and refugee situations.

Aid workers are required to consult with the local community to find out how they can best help them.

For details please contact:

Australian Committee for UNICEF Ltd
ACN 060 581 437
P O Box K 485 Haymarket NSW 2000 or
G P O Box 9911 in your capital city

UNICEF is an Equal Opportunity Employer

WORLD VISION AUSTRALIA
World Vision of Australia - A C N 004 778 081

Wanted: Global Aid Worker

World Vision of Australia is looking for interested Australian staff to work alongside local people in projects in Somalia, India, Guatemala and Bangladesh.

Doctors, nurses, accountants, engineers, agriculturalists and teachers are needed.

For details please contact:

World Vision of Australia

GPO Box 9944
in your capital city

(1996) Global Education Resource

Activity Sheet 5.4

The work of global aid workers

Global aid workers	What we knew at the start	What we found out after research
Country of origin (Where do they come from?)		
Qualifications (What skills and training do they need?)		
Experience (What work have they done?)		
Organisations (Which organisations do they work for?)		
Situations (What kind of situations mean communities need aid?)		
Destinations (Where do they work? Which countries are receiving aid?)		

UNICEF Australia Projects 1992–1993

LEBANON

IMMUNISATION – $50,000

Source of funds: AusAID

During the past decade the number of child deaths from immunisable diseases has been dramatically reduced. This has been achieved through vaccines for measles, tuberculosis (BCG) and other diseases in children during their first year of life.

The Australian contribution is providing vaccines and essential drugs. A matching contribution has been provided by the Lebanese community in Australia.

PHILIPPINES

STREET CHILDREN – $17,530

Source of funds: AusAID

An estimated 120,000-150,000 children live and forage for their survival on the streets in major cities in the Philippines.

This project aims to gather the information needed to develop support programs for these children.

The information needed includes interviews with children, ways they can be assisted, counselling for sexually exploited and abused children and strategies to combat drug dependency and help street children who break the law.

AusAID provided funds to enable UNICEF Australia to collect and analyse data on street children and to prepare a strategy. A major project will be implemented over the period 1993-1996 with funds provided by AusAID.

SOUTH PACIFIC

SOCIAL MOBILISATION – $270,000

Source of funds: AusAID

The social and economic structure in the South Pacific is changing rapidly. At one extreme are traditional extended families who provide for all their own needs at the local level. At the other extreme are urban nuclear families who work for wages and need to buy goods and services.

Significant strides in primary health care and immunisation have been made, but currently over 9000 Pacific Island children die each year in their first year of life.

Dealing with change requires the use of government and community resources to bring about adequate health care, nutrition, education and an environment that supports the well-being of children.

The purpose of this project is to support and accelerate UNICEF's work with Pacific that focuses on helping children.

UNICEF Australia Projects 1992–1993

VIETNAM

BASIC EDUCATION FOR ETHNIC MINORITIES – $151,086

Source of funds: AusAID and UNICEF Australia

The aim of this project is to improve the basic education of children from ethnic minorities and other disadvantaged children in remote areas of Vietnam.

Through high failure and drop-out rates, less than 10% of children who live in remote areas throughout Vietnam complete primary education.

Teaching materials and training programs will upgrade the skills of existing teachers. Suitably qualified ethnic minority students will also be selected for special training programs to equip them with skills to teach ethnic minority children in small schools in their own regions.

ZIMBABWE

WATER AND SANITATION – $474,830

Source of funds: AusAID

This project focuses on the Beitbridge District, one of the poorest regions in Zimbabwe. Water and sanitation facilities in the region are extremely limited.

Large numbers of people are forced to use unsafe water; consequently, the incidence of disease is extremely high and is the principal cause of infant deaths in the district.

The primary goal is to reduce the number of deaths of young children and is to be achieved through the provision of clean water, sanitation facilities and hygiene education for the local population.

(1996) Global Education Resource

Topic 2 Working together – How can we help?

Teaching and learning activities

1 Ask students to visualise a better world, in groups, pairs or individually. They can focus on a country or specific issue (ie famine, floods, homelessness). They should draw the world they foresee and then use arrows and label the improvements (eg everyone has running water).

2 Ask students, in small groups to brainstorm a list of ways they could make a better world. Have them write these as short explanatory statements, beginning with "If we … then …".

3 Explain to students that the video *World Vision Education,* Section 6, 'Bridging cooperation: Helping people help themselves' will provide further information about global aid work to assist them in constructing an explanation text. Ask students to take notes on:

a) What members of the community did
b) What World Vision workers did
c) What changes took place

Remind students that when recording information they should take notes using bullet points and be as brief as possible, recording key words or phrases, just enough to convey meaning.

4 As a whole class discuss after viewing.

Focus Questions

What was the community's need? How did building the bridge assist the community? How did community members work to meet their community's needs? Who assisted the community, and in what ways?

As a whole class summarise information under headings generated by the discussion. These headings can then be used as the basis for developing paragraphs in an explanation.

5 Provide some model texts of explanations for students. Show them that explanations are used to account for how something works or provide reasons for an event or phenomenon. Use the model texts to highlight language features, such as

- generalised non-human participants (the bridge, the war, the village)
- cause and effect relationships (because, so, if, as a result, due to, because of this, since, consequently)
- temporal relationships (following, then, finally, before)
- mainly action verbs (builds, assists, carries)
- timeless (simple) present tense

(adapted Derewianka 1990: 62)

6. Explain to students that the first or topic sentence of each paragraph should indicate what is to come in that paragraph. Also explain that the order in which information is given within the sentence is very important. For instance, when writing a paragraph about the building of the bridge, the paragraph should have a topic sentence that begins with the most important element, eg 'The bridge building *started* on Thursday and all the villagers came to help'.

   Point out to students that this sentence indicates that what is to follow in the paragraph will concern the building of the bridge, not 'the villagers' or 'Thursday'. This will support students to avoid beginning sentences with 'All the villagers…', 'They started…' or 'On Thursday…'

7. Divide students into small groups. Ask each group to write a concise topic sentence which could begin a paragraph which will answer the following questions:

   - What was the community's need?
   - What did World Vision workers do?
   - What did members of the community do?
   - How did building the bridge assist the community?
   - How did community members work to meet their community's needs?
   - Who assisted the community, and in what ways?
   - What changes took place?

8. Have groups swap their topic sentence for editing. They should read the topic sentence and highlight the most important or relevant element in each sentence and return it to its writers.

9. Each group can then rewrite their topic sentences ensuring the most important element appears at the beginning of the sentence. This is called the 'theme position' in a sentence.

10. Write up each group's topic sentence.

11. Display **Activity Sheet 5.6** which will support students to plan and write their final explanation of the project.

12. Remind students of the features of the explanation structure on **Activity Sheet 5.6**. Then ask them what order the topic sentences from Activity 7 should be in. Ask them to provide reasons. Make changes to the sequence of the topic sentences as suggested by students and the explanation structure.

13. Using **Activity Sheet 5.6**, jointly construct a topic sentence to describe what the aid project is. Prompt students by asking them questions such as 'What is it?' 'Where is it?'. Point out that you are using timeless (simple) present tense. Ask students whether the most important element of the sentence appears at the beginning.

14. Ask students to use their notes from the class discussion and the video to complete the explanation using the prompts on the sheet. This could be done in pairs or independently.

15. Encourage students to draw a flow chart diagram explaining the best solution for the problem put forward in their explanation. Ensure that you have modelled a flow chart for them.

Activity Sheet 5.6

Explanation

Statement of phenomenon

Aid project (use present tense, describe the project. What is it? Where is it?)

What is the problem? (why is the project needed?)

Explanation sequence (what are the causes and effects of the problem? Explain how and why the problem arose and show the relationship between cause and effect by using some causal conjunctions/connectives such as: because, so, as a result, due to, because of this, consequently)

What are some of the solutions for the problem? (how can the problem start to be solved straight away, and in the future?)

Short term solutions:

Long term solutions:

RESOURCES

(1996) *Global Education Resource*. Sydney: AUSAID, UNICEF Australia, World Vision, Australia and the NSW Department of School Education.

(1999) *Access Asia: Primary Teaching and Learning Units*. Carlton, Vic: Curriculum Corporation.

(1999) *Look Global: Global Perspectives in the Upper Primary Classroom*. Carlton, Vic: Curriculum Corporation.

(1999) *Think Global: Global Education for the Early Years*. Carlton, Vic: Curriculum Corporation.

Gilligan, Beth (1999) *Voice and Values: Citizenship in Asia*. Carlton, Vic: Curriculum Corporation.

Hamston J, Pidgon, K & Woolley, M (1999) *To Market*. Carlton, Vic: Curriculum Corporation.

www.amnesty.com	Amensty International
www.unicef.com.au	UNICEF Australia
www.worldvision.org	World Vision
www.care.org	Care Australia
www.austcare.com.au	Austcare
www.msf.org	Medecins Sans Frontieres

BIBLIOGRAPHY AND FURTHER READING

(1999) *Aspire: 2000 Olympic Games Resource for Australian Schools*. NSW Depatment of Education and Training, Curriculum Corporation & University of Wollongong.

(1998) *Clean Air 2000: An NRMA initiative*. National Curriculum Services.

(November 1999) *The Daily Telegraph – Sydney, a celebration in pictures*. A millennium special, Parts 1-6.

(1997) *Oodles of Noodles: Early Years Integrated Units Collection*. Carlton, Vic: Curriculum Corporation.

(1995) 'Reading cereal boxes: analysing everyday texts R-5 unit' in *Texts: The heart of the English curriculum Series 1*, Curriculum Division, Department of Education and Children's Services, South Australia.

(1994) *Studies of Society and Environment: A statement on studies of Society and Environment for Australian Schools.* Victoria: Curriculum Corporation.

Butt D, Fahey R, Spinks S & Yallop C (1995) *Using functional grammar: An explorer's guide*, Sydney: NCELTR Macquarie University.

Callow J (1999) *Image matters: Visual texts in the classroom*. Sydney: PETA.

Collerson, J (1997) *Grammar in teaching*, Sydney: PETA

Colerson J (1994) *English grammar: A functional approach*. PETA: Sydney.

Creenaune, T & Rowles L (1996) *What's your purpose: Reading strategies for non-fiction texts*. Sydney: PETA.

Department of Employment, Education and Training (1995) *Langwij comes to school*, Canberra: DEET.

Derewianka, B (1998) *A Grammar Companion for Primary Teachers*. Sydney: PETA.

Derewianka, B (1990) *Exploring How Texts Work*. Sydney: PETA.

Eades D (1993) *Aboriginal English*. PEN 93. Sydney: PETA.

Eggins S and Slade D (1997) *Analysing Casual Conversatio*n. London: Cassell.

Halliday, M A K (1985) *An Introduction to Functional Grammar*, London: Edward Arnold.

Halliday, M A K (1985) *Spoken and Written Language*, Victoria: Deakin University Press.

Hillel M & Mappin A (1995) *Choosing and Using Literature*. Carlton, Vic: Curriculum Corporation.

Jones, P (ed) *Talking to Learn*. Sydney: PETA.

Hook, C (1999) *Learning in the Museum* PEN 121. Sydney: PETA.

Horton, D (Editor) (1994) *Encyclopedia of Aboriginal Australia: Aboriginal and Torres Strait Islander History, Society and Culture*, Canberra: Aboriginal Studies Press for Australian Institute of Aboriginal and Torres Strait Islander Studies.

Hunt, I (1994) *Successful Joint Construction* PEN 96. Sydney: PETA.

Lewis M & Wray D (1999) *Writing in the curriculum: Frames to support learning*. Sydney: PETA.

Martin, JR (1992) *English Text*. Amsterdam: John Benjamins B.V.

Martin J & Rothery J (1980) *Writing Project Report No. 1.* Sydney: Department of Linguistics, University of Sydney.

Martin J & Rothery J (1981) *Writing Project Report No. 2*. Sydney: Department of Linguistics, University of Sydney.

Martin J & Rothery J (1986) *Writing Project Report No. 4.* Sydney: Department of Linguistics, University of Sydney.

Number 7: Australia's Prime Ministers. Sydney: Australian Knowledge.

Robinson P (1999) *This fantastic century: Worksheets.* Queensland: Queensland Newspapers Pty Ltd.

Schmidt A (1990) *The loss of Australia's Aboriginal language heritage*, Canberra: Aboriginal Studies Press for Australian Institute for Aboriginal and Torres Strait Islander Studies.

Social education in the nineties: A basic right for every person, Sydney: Social Education Association of Australia.

The Snowy Mountains scheme The power of water A teacher resource guide. Snowy Mountains Hydro-Electric Authority.

Wray D & Lewis M (1997) Teaching factual writing: Purpose and structure. *Australian Journal of Language and Literacy*. Vol 20. No 2.